THE SECOND LIFE OF JUDO

Published by:

Farfallina Press

MLG & Associates
Farfallina Press
66 Witherspoon Street, Suite 115
Princeton, NJ 08542
www.mlgpubgroup.com

Cover & interior design by Jill Abrahamsen
Illustrations by Arant Creative Group
ISBN: 9780984550753
Library of Congress Control Number: 2012936022

THE SECOND LIFE OF JUDO

WHEN FLESH IS FILLED WITH SPIRIT

ALAN RAFKIND

Published by Farfallina Press

To My Wife Gina,

To My Dog Roxy, My Family and Friends,

My Spiritual Teacher Teresa, Mr. Richard Bennett,

William R. Huff & Cathy Markey Huff,

Cheri Huber, Bill Martin, Scott Asalone,

Marie Galastro and Arant Creative Group –

A Deep Bow of Thanks

Preface

I did not discover Judo through my own volition. My father Don was pretty straightforward about why he carted my brother Mike and me – at the ages of eight and six – to the local dojo no more than five or six miles from our house in Matawan, New Jersey. Over the years, I must have heard my father repeat his standard line a hundred times. When asked how my brother and I got involved in the sport, he would say, "I am small and their mother is small, so I knew my kids were going to be small. I thought it would be a good idea for them to learn how to protect themselves." Growing up playing on the streets of Brooklyn, NY in the late 1940's, my father really knew only one answer to the schoolyard bully. It was the old-school mentality of "Hit first in the nose, and hit as hard as you can." When my brother and I were young, our father still knew nothing about the martial arts, or the differences between them. But one day, he saw that the local dojo offered Judo classes, starting at both 5pm and 6pm, and he decided to sign us up. My father worked in New York City, and these were simply the only times he could get back home to sit and watch his boys in class.

Like most kids, my initial goals were to climb the ladder of belt colors and win tournaments. I soon discovered that both were not easy tasks. All martial art practices require you to make friends with Father Time. Belt promotions are not given frequently in Judo, and as they say, there is always someone out there who takes winning a bit more seriously than you do.

Starting at eight years old did give me an advantage, however. Many techniques became as natural as riding a bike. There is a quality of a 'natural' technique that I can only describe as a technique that moves you, rather than you conduct the technique. Through my teenage years and my twenties, the belts came and the trophies appeared, but there was a missing ingredient for me. I almost quit a couple of times, as I unsuccessfully attempted to corral this intangible ingredient. I got caught up in wanting new, different, and advanced techniques, in the effort to avoid the monotonous repetition of the basics. Thankfully my teacher Richard Bennett knew the correct pace for me. He knew that if I moved too quickly to the more advanced techniques, my general skill set would falter. He also knew that if I didn't taste the more advanced techniques, my general interest would fade.

From the very first time I stepped into a dojo, I felt something religious and spiritual from the environment and practice. This was the mystery ingredient, and is the one that fills the flesh with spirit. If I could paint a picture of this ingredient it would look like 'humility meeting harmony,' whatever you imagine that to look like. As a youngster, all I knew was that being in the dojo felt good and comfortable. It was a place for me where the struggle of daily life seemed to drop away. Now, 30 years later, the real gift of the martial arts is the "easy-going, centered state of being" lived outside the dojo in all of my life experiences.

I am so grateful to my mom for rounding my brother and I up with clean judogi's in hand and carting us over to the dojo three or four times a week. I am so grateful to my father for getting us involved in this life-changing sport. Without them, this book would have never been written.

June 3, 2009, Matawan, New Jersey

Table of Contents

Table of Contents

Introduction

This book honors the Spiritual Art born out of the Mother School in 1882, which has spread to the city and country dojos throughout the world. I dedicate this guide book to the courageous Judokas who have walked through the front door of a dojo and to their whole initial experience: stepping barefoot onto the mat, being thrown down countless times, tapping their partner to convey submission, deciding to get up and show up for the next class and to do it all again.

You can walk into any bookstore across the country, go to the Martial Arts section and find at least a couple of books on the topic of Judo – primarily what we call the "First Life of Judo." These books will neatly lay out instruction on numerous techniques and use numerous pictures to outline movements broken down by intermittent hip, arm, and foot positions. They may even contain a few fun facts about tournament play, the originators of the art, and more.

Beyond the First Life of Judo being an Olympic sport and a means of self-defense, Judo is a way of living and interacting with life, and simultaneously, it's a way of allowing life to interact with you. The Second Life of Judo is a life practice, one which is too fluid and integrative for 'brute force' to touch. For many people, Judo starts out as a martial art, only to transform itself into a spiritual art. Each and every one of us has a warrior's heart for acceptance, and that is all we ever need to enter into the Second Life of Judo.

The First Life of Judo is played out with thousands of repetitions and the quest for students to become athletic champions. This life is more concerned with patches of victory sewed onto a uniform and trophies added to a shelf. If you are lucky, the First Life of Judo will last 35 years, and if you are not so lucky, it will last a lifetime.

My personal transformation started happening soon after I was awarded a Black Belt in September 1991. Representatives from the United States Judo Association (U.S.J.A.) came to my teachers' dojo, the P.J.K. Professional Judo and Karate School in Matawan, NJ, to conduct my test. My belt ultimately spent more time hanging in the closet than around my waist. The testosterone-filled nights were instead gladly left to the green and brown belts trying to establish themselves as formidable up-and-comers. I, however, became less and less interested in how much weight I could lift and more interested in how much weight I could bear. Similarly, I became less interested in muscle strength and more interested in inner strength. I wondered: Who lives with a great sense of well-being, and who celebrates life, even during extremely difficult situations? A softening process had begun for me. Life was filled with a new-found acceptance in my becoming more attuned to my relation to everything. With continued and unconditional acceptance came a deep strength within.

Unwavering acceptance is a lasting source of power that cannot be matched by an exhaustible bicep muscle of an opponent. A maturation process was indeed taking place. Judo became more about embracing partners than throwing them. The Black Belt signified the wisdom that comes with allowing life to unfold in all its unpredictable ways. This was my driving force. I was being inducted into the Second Life of Judo.

"That which we force will react, that which we guide will respond."

"**Kneel** to no one, bow to few, stand with all"

THE PRACTICE

COOPERATION

In Judo play, when we move left, our partners move left. When our partners reduce the pressure of their grip, we tend do the same. We know when our partners give up all hopes of escaping our hold, and they know the same when we give up. Between two partners, feet, legs, hips, torsos, arms, and even thoughts become like one. As our partners practice a technique, we release our defensive postures so that they can experience entries, turns, and lifts with freedom. During Uchi Komi (repetitive fitting drill to develop skill), we allow our partners to feel their technique and movements in full.

Practice Judo long enough and a transformation will take place. Judokas transform from being tight to relaxed, constricted to expansive, heavy to light, shrinking to spacious, and fearful to fearless. Becoming vulnerable indicates one's practice is growing strong. We are learning to respond to whatever may come.

In class, we are paired up as Uke (technique receiver) and Tori (technique performer). For example, the Tori is the one who throws; the Uke is the one who is thrown. Uke and Tori cooperate with one another, to their mutual benefit. We are encouraged to rotate partners to experience different styles of play. Not everyone we partner with will work at our pace or with our intensity – maybe it will be more or less.

We learn to work closely with all types of people: the lazy, the motivated, the strong, the weak, the big, the small, the Asian, the African-American, the fragile, and the rugged. What better way to learn how to cooperate with others?

Of course, there is vocal instruction from the head sensei, but practice is conducted mostly in silence, except for the sound of Break Falls, breathing, movement counts, and body contact. No matter which position is yours, Uke or Tori, you rely on your partner for your own improvement in technique and stamina. There is an unspoken language between partners that says, "Thank you for being here for me to push, pull, hook, sweep, block, lift, and twist. I will do the very same for you in return." This unwritten agreement states, "I will treat your body as sacred as my own." The partners take care of each other, and a sacrifice is made for each other. This is the spirit of companionship. We are willing to travel together, despite any differences. It's the traveling that joins us as brothers and sisters of the art. We support our practice partner in the way that we want to be supported. Everything that we give is given in the Second Life of Judo. There is nothing left to do but continue to treat one another as we wish to be treated. This is the 'Gentle Way.'

"In the Second Life of Judo, we display a sense of gratitude for our practice partner outside the dojo – our Uki and Tori of life."

THE BLACK BELT

In all spiritual arts, one's skill level or physical strength is never measured with more importance than in how we interact with one another. The Second Life of Judo is a proving ground for integrity, a place where character matters. It matters so much, that the rank one attains is a reflection of character more than anything else. It can be said that the deeper the color belt the practitioners wear, the deeper they have opened their hearts to compassion and kindness. In the Second Life of Judo, one does not need to wear a Judo belt at all to display character – just being human will suffice.

There is an ancient saying in the martial arts. It says that every time participants tighten their obi (belts), they are reminded to generate the courage of the gut upward in order to pierce the muscle of the heart. The action (of tightening the belt) is a constant reminder that we must use our courage and strength in a compassionate manner, and to do our best to live a life of non-violence and do no harm. It's also a perfect reminder because the knot of the obi becomes loose over and over again, and is always in need of a tug to keep it tight and to keep the belt from falling off the body.

Breaking boards and winning tournaments are fun to do, but they are over-rated. Ten-year-old Black Belts are being set up with a false concept of a spiritual art. True spiritual power can never come from awards or rewards. These will, however, reinforce the false concept that we have to fight one another in order to accomplish this power. When this is the case, you become a weapon of hate, and you will need to practice with your brother's and sister's of the art to sharpen your skills with the intention of not hurting one another. In so doing, you transform movement into a Martial Art Form.

Today, it is common to see one opponent beat down another inside a cage or a ring. Any activity with the sole intention of harming or injuring another is not a spiritual art. There is nothing honorable in drawing blood for a contract, for entertainment, or to prove that one's physical strength and style of combat is superior to another's.

I was fortunate enough to practice at a dojo with mat space big enough to conduct tournaments. Competitors from the Tri-State area were classified by age, weight, and rank. Competitors young and old had at least two matches, regardless of whether they won or lost. At the end of competition, the tournament director would make it a point to recognize each and every Judoka that participated. If a Judoka lost both matches, he or she would not leave empty-handed. All competitors were given the same ribbon for participating. During the award ceremony, every competitor was called front and center to accept a handshake and a bow of recognition for competing. The dojo makes a point not to put anyone too high or too low on a pedestal. The dojo teaches unity.

The intention set forth is to have every adult or child, regardless of rank, take part in a Judo tournament experience and realize that winning or losing was by far secondary to participating. Young players would eat oranges together, tighten each other's belts, and take turns throwing a bean bag onto the mat (so the referee knew when time ran out during matches). This is what makes tournaments fun.

There is a true story of a very special sensei. This sensei was known as a teacher's teacher, because many very experienced judokas would take his class to learn all the minor details of the most advanced techniques. He was one of the highest-ranking Judokas in the whole country.

This sensei had an illustrious Judo career; he had won an All-Japan title. He later came to the U.S. to devote his life to teaching. One day on a whim, he decided to enter a tournament on the very day that the tournament was taking place. As his students grabbed their judogis (uniforms) and headed over to the tournament location, much to their surprise, their great sensei was following right along with his Gi (short name for uniform) in hand. Everyone's eyes were glued to this man, knowing they would soon get a chance to see this great man in action. This sensei proceeded to win all his matches in stunning fashion, leading up to the finals. As expected, all his matches up to that point looked like a mere warm up to him, for Judo was in his blood. Then, in the final match, everyone gasped, as they watched this great sensei get caught in his less experienced opponent's technique. All the witnesses felt a rush of unease roll over them – they had been sure this man was unbeatable. His students in particular felt as if his reputation and his school's reputation had just suffered a crushing blow. One student said, "I feel embarrassed for him." The legacy of this master seemed to be abruptly ending at a mere competition, not even a national tournament. But then, something very amazing happened. This sensei displayed his humble character. He went right over to the competitor who beat him and said, "Excuse me, that was a fantastic technique. Would you be kind enough to show me how you did that?" In that moment, he taught everyone that it is a great act of courage and inner strength to lose with honor, and respect carrying a beginner's mind. Needless to say, this special sensei remained a teacher's teacher!

"Kneel to No One, Bow to Few, Stand with All"

THE ESSENCE OF TRADITION

In the 80's, my teacher Mr. Bennett made a bold and courageous decision in the name of the spiritual art of Judo. He decided to bring the very core teachings of the art out into the public. Our school went out to county fairs, high schools, parks, and malls to display and demonstrate my teacher's vision of making Judo accessible to anyone and everyone. Mr. B's demonstrations were not always accepted by peers and other instructors, to say the least. The very act of bringing the techniques outside the dojo was frowned upon by many traditional teachers. But anyone who truly knows my teacher knows that peer pressure and degradation from others would not dissuade him. And many people, including myself, are extremely thankful that Mr. B was not discouraged.

Mr. B knew that there was no conflict of interest in performing demonstrations. He knew that the quality of Judo would remain at the very highest level. He knew that providing this experience to the public through his students – and himself – would actually enhance the name and versatility of the art. I know that demonstration, practice, and performance made me a more complete Judoka. On top of that, it was fun! Mr. B knew that fun and practice go hand and hand; they are two sides to the same helpful coin.

Even with the use of more "non-traditional" props, like mini trampolines, music, and costumes, the integrity of the art was never once compromised in the name of entertainment. In reality, the true teachings of Judo, such as flexibility in muscle tissue, lifestyle, style of play, and teaching structure were expressed in my teacher's decision to have his school perform demonstrations. As his student, I was hearing the subliminal message: "Okay, I have this very special art to offer, and I have this blank slate of possibility, with many options in how to do it." Mr. B lived from the place of possibility and creativity. Whether you take a Judo class in New Jersey, California, or Tokyo, you can expect it to be comprised of similar traditional components but every sensei brings his own particular style, personality, humor, intensity and warmth to the class.

*"Spirit guides the body like writing heartfelt poetry
guides the fingers."*

YIN AND YANG

*"Heaviness — and the location closer to the ground giving more
stability — is Yin, while lightness — and the location closer to Heaven,
giving more freedom in movements — is Yang."*
— Dr. Joseph Kim

Experienced Judokas adjust and shift their body weight effectively to hold down their partners. If we invest too much downward Yin energy we can be rolled by our partner. If we invest in too much Yang energy and space for observation, our partner will have room to escape. Therefore, we become very aware of the power we have from this place called "the center."

There are Yin qualities in Yang positions, and Yang qualities in Yin positions. The most efficient ground holds consist of a mixture of both Yin and Yang energies. When we hold our partners down, our upper body weight remains heavy with "pressing down" energy (Yin). The very same hold requires a slightly lighter energy (Yang) in our legs. A lighter, lower body base enables us to adjust our legs in order to stabilize our body weight and steady our partner's movements.

When we rely too much on Yang principles, we are aggressively attempting to force movements, and we will find ourselves too far off center (and will likely get countered). Similarly, a Judoka who stubbornly strives to complete the same technique over and over again when his partner clearly sees it coming is playing too much Yang-based Judo, which is ultimately not effective.

When we rely too much on Yin principles, based on inactivity and a "fortress-like" defense, we will also find ourselves off center, and we perform like a song that sounds flat. Judokas who start their techniques but remain skittish and who immediately come back to their defensive base time and time again, are playing exclusively Yin-based Judo (also not effective). When observing Yin and Yang principles, we balance our minds and bodies equally.

As our Judo matures, we learn to trust the principles of Yin and Yang. Judo is a strong teacher of this principle, because the experience is felt with our whole body. The First Life of Judo is a literal teacher of balance. You move this way or that with your body weight – and you either end up on your back, or you remain standing and flexible, like bamboo. The Second Life of Judo teaches what it means to have a flexible state of mind. We learn to silence the mind and relax the body. This practice produces the exact amount of energy we need.

We never have to step foot in a dojo to live the principles of Yin and Yang. Riding a horse, swimming in the ocean, or bowling are all great teachers of "center." Our everyday tasks can also teach us about being centered, if we listen. Without awareness of this principle, we find ourselves pulled by the undertow and dragged one hundred yards off shore. Learning about Yin and Yang is learning to live in harmony with our surroundings. Of course we find ourselves off-center from time to time, but we then adjust and do what is necessary to come back. You'll find that if you release your grip slightly, you will be okay. This is how we relax and routinely return to our center.

Have you ever gone tubing? First, you sit inside a big inner tube. You begin upstream, and you allow the running water to float you downstream. You may bounce off a boulder; you may get going faster than you prefer in strong rapids; you may float into a still pool where paddling is necessary; or you may enjoy a steadily paced ride for an hour. Center is a place where there is no struggle in the experience. Nothing is therefore labeled as a problem, no matter where the current takes you. Being in harmony with the flow of life best describes this place.

"When you're centered, do you now feel the peace within the chaos?"

NO CONTROL

Are you willing to take the role of student and allow the Universe to be the sensei? Allowing the sensei in the dojo to dictate what comes is good acceptance practice. Sooner is better than later to realize that the Universe is in control. After all, the Universe is our sensei. We have no real control over our finances, health, relationships, family, or the actions of loved ones. Everything we experience is impermanent and in a constant state of flux. Control can never be applied to movement and change. Impossible! This rule of the dojo applies to everything. We soon learn the difference between force and power. When we apply force, we are trying to control the outcome. But we possess our truest power when no force is being applied.

The judogi material is made from very strongly stitched fibers. The gi is made to endure years of pulling, twisting, gripping and friction. Consequently, the human skin is no match for a gi. When playing Judo, we are reminded of this difference over and over again, as we learn to quit trying to control our partner and their movements. A gi burn looks like a four-inch welt or abrasion on the skin. Resist your partner's movements too much and you will get burnt; and if your partner is strong, you will bleed. A judogi burn goes away in a few days, and we get another chance to recognize the need to relax and move fluidly with our partner's energy and weight.

This is a friendly reminder to let go of control and lighten up our tendency to resist, for the Universe does not revolve around our preferences. The sun and ocean tides have rhythms of their own. Invest too much of your mental energy in controlling the uncontrollable, and you may experience a more harmful reminder. This ego-driven stress may ultimately wind you up in a hospital, or prevent you from getting out of bed. You may even experience a near-fatal reminder, such as a stroke or heart attack. Unfortunately then, you may never get another chance to experience this precious life with a relaxed spirit.

"That which we force will react. That which we guide will respond."

My teacher says, "Judo makes everything else in life easier." I didn't understand this Zen Koan at first, but I see its meaning now: Life can be difficult. Being human comes with any number of difficult realities: a stressful job, a natural disaster, or a health crisis, to name a few. Judo is much more than movement and exercise. Yes, it feels good to breathe heavily, to sweat and release pent-up energy. But Judo is an activity that teaches us the value of non-resistance. Non-resistance is a deeper layer of practice that all spiritual arts offer. Becoming aware of resistance is enlightening. Whether we shoot an arrow at a target, paint a picture, or diet to lose weight, we receive valuable lessons about resistance and control – when we pay attention. We excel in arts when we drop resistance, right here and right now.

Whether he's in the dojo or on his farm, Mr. B maintains an unwavering level of acceptance. He tells me, "I use my Judo to get the horses in the trailer." I laugh, because I know the Judo he refers to is logical, adaptive, relative to everything, and does not mean relying on force. There is no forcing a 1,000-pound animal, such as a horse, to do what it refuses to do. Instead, Mr. B gently guides his horses in a roundabout pattern. Feeling no resistance and with the flow of their own momentum, the horses relax and enter the trailer. The Second Life of Judo is about embracing the moment, and allowing wisdom and the power of possibility to emerge in all experiences.

"We allow, and then respond, with our whole being" would be a good motto to describe both the manner in which Mr. B lives and how he plays Judo. Like the classic Zen paradox, Mr. B accomplishes through the path of least resistance. The path of least resistance is not always the easiest. This creative 'guidance' instinct which leads us to the path of least resistance takes time to cultivate. Until then, the stages of development usually come with lessons on patience.

We have been so conditioned to "do more" that doing less is not as easy as it sounds. We have been so conditioned to "do things our way," that doing something else is also not easy at first. Do not mistake the path of least resistance for a lack of enthusiasm. It is quite the opposite. It is a path that requires our undivided attention and consistent practice. It has been described as a path we walk daily, but seemingly we go nowhere. Actually, there is no place to go. We realize that we are in the only place that we will ever be – Here!

THE GENTLE WAY

By nature, Judo is physical, and the dynamics of the sport are extremely complex to master. Judo play is rooted in anatomy, physiology and engineering. The transfer of energy between two individuals dictates all the movements. We become much like containers that capture and receive flowing water, and then these same containers become upright, spilling over at the right time and at the right angle. The water in this example above symbolizes an opponent's body weight and energy. This is the philosophy behind all movements in Judo. This philosophy has everything to do with abiding and yielding to a partner's energy, and nothing to do with controlling him. This is why the word Judo translates as "The Gentle Way."

In the dojo, we learn not to "ride high on the horse." We learn not to become full of ourselves, nor exaggerate the invincible and bullying ways of our ego. When we do ride too high, we are brought down to earth, literally and metaphorically. The dojo is a place where everyone, despite their best efforts, gets brought down to earth. On the mat, we get knocked off our feet, and we must stand up time and time again. We learn to cultivate the self-support we need to relax and respond from under hard places. Through this process, there is a dying of the ego over and over again, resulting in an outlook of hard work and humility. No one gets exactly what they want or prefer most of the time, in the dojo or in life, so acceptance and kindness are the only answers. Acceptance and kindness are qualities which do not crumble when things get heavy . . . like a container that removes its weight and remains buoyant.

UNIQUE TECHNIQUE

When we accept ourselves exactly the way we are, it becomes very clear where (and how) we can apply effort in training. Some Judokas who are physically strong will be naturally attracted to pulling and lifting techniques in their play. It is important that these same able-bodied players practice finesse techniques to improve their timing. This will give the physically strong players a more complete game. Some long-limbed Judokas, on the other hand, will be attracted to leverage movements, such as Foot Sweeps, Hooking Throws, and Reaping Throws. They will have to balance out their Judo game by sharpening techniques that require unsuspected bursts of strength. Shorter Judokas may want to use their proximity to the ground to their advantage with "dropping" techniques. But even short Judokas must still become excellent at leverage movements. Judokas who rush into a technique will practice patience by spending a bit more time setting up offensive movements.

Judokas who are known for fast and explosive entries can play from a distance that suits their speed. A slower Judoka, however, may want to use deception to gain access and close the distance to an opponent, much like the insect that draws its prey close by remaining camouflaged. But both fast and slower Judokas must practice playing from all distances, both spacious and tight. In Judo, as in life, we can't always ride the wave of just what comes easy. Accept who you are, and your Judo becomes great.

When we accept who we are, we see where our spiritual work lies. It is good practice for individuals who are impatient to sit in traffic or wait on a slow-moving line. It is wonderful practice for an individual who has an aversion to cold to shovel snow. It is great practice for those that have a deep-seated fear of water to stand in the shallow end of the pool, to slowly learn to relax, and lastly to move away from the wall. Avoid this beneficial work if you must, but soon enough, the Universe will put that metaphorical stick out in front of your shins. If we take notice, the Universe often provides us with what we need to evolve spiritually.

"Suffering has a noble purpose – the evolution of consciousness and the burning up of the ego."
– Eckhart Tolle

HANDS-FREE JUDO

A misconception about Judo is that the physicality of the art is equal to violence and aggressive behavior. In reality, if you see an advanced spiritual artist practice, you will see an inherit energy of kindness and care generating all the Judo master's movements. To be kind is to celebrate the core teachings of all the spiritual arts. An individual who practices a martial art for the purpose of inflating the ego or injuring another has not even come close to understanding the art. All spiritual arts are created equal, in this respect.

The first rule of the martial arts is to 'walk away' from any possible physical confrontation not begun in the name of sportsmanship and companionship. This rule is expressed frequently by reputable instructors. We become spiritual artists, in fact, at those times when we feel the heat of anger coursing through our veins, and yet we are still led by a greater awareness to walk away from hostile confrontations. We are mindful of this dilemma when we practice diffusing situations full of aggression and tension. If we are being bullied, or a friend is being bullied, we can likely diffuse the situation with words. With a lot of practice we now trust ourselves to set a clear verbal and emotional tone and respond wholeheartedly to whatever the situation may dictate. With such an awareness leading the way, we can stand up for someone who is weak or less capable of standing up for himself. The ultimate expression of self-defense is when we act as the catalyst for both the bully and the bullied, to allow them both to walk away unharmed. This way, both people get another chance to transform. We train and become comfortable with the physical, in order to stand in the name of non-violence. In the martial arts, the physical aspect and the spiritual aspect lie within each other. When you progress in the arts, your physical actions represent your core values.

When the internally strong stands up for the physically or internally weak, each becomes stronger and more empowered. How does one accomplish this? It's called 'hands-free Judo.' This Judo is displayed in the words and tones we choose to use. Hands-free Judo is a deep inner confidence, expressed in the willingness to keep a situation from ever reaching the point of verbal abuse or physical violence. The "Black Belt" in hands-free Judo provides an environment for aggressive energy to dissolve, or else move away in a safe manner. Practitioners of hands-free Judo create this space and setting with humility and are skillful and creative in responding in ways that are non-threatening. When an individual is bullied with words like, "I can kick your ass, punk," a hands-free Judo response may be, "I'm sure you can." Hands-free Judo is evident in one's tone of voice, even more than in the actual words used. It's the tone that conveys a clear but relaxed message, leaving a fearless impression.

One who practices hands-free Judo receives and absorbs energy without resistance – therefore, energy is transformed. Whether this transformation takes place physically in a dojo or verbally in a school yard, it is still Judo. Make no mistake, hands-free Judo is a powerful response and is by all definitions, a true art of self-defense. This is what the spiritually advanced can do for someone who is having a hard time. This is what someone did for me once, when I was having a difficult time. They were present for me. They listened to me. It only makes sense for me to do the same for others.

In the Second Life of Judo, we display a sense of gratitude for our practice partner outside the dojo – our Uki and Tori of life.

"Love is the highest principle of the Martial Arts."

— Morihei Ueshiba

THE ART

RELAX

Both Uke and Tori realize that when their muscles are tight and stiff, their movements are restricted. Also, they tire more quickly, and there is a greater chance of becoming injured. As Judokas, we quickly learn that offensive and defensive movements are most effective when we neither cling onto our partners too tightly, nor push them away too vigorously. Often, a beginner Judoka will attempt to hold a partner at bay by using a stiff-arm position, as well as with a clenched grip. The beginner soon realizes that this posture actually inhibits movement. When the grip is too tight and the wrists, elbows, and shoulders are rigid, it is extremely difficult to enter into a throwing technique. These beginners often lock themselves out of offensive movements with a guarded stiff-arm posture. On the other side of the coin, it is no fun for someone with a rigid body position to be thrown; they hit the mat like a two-by-four, instead of landing like a water balloon. A water balloon landing is much more preferable – there is more give when one hits the surface of the mat.

During Mr. B's class, he would repeat often to "stand up more straight and relax your stance." When we are loose and open, we can feel our rib cage floating, which enables air to easily enter our lungs. Our head is up, our gaze is wide, and our elbow and knee joints are soft. We learn to breathe in rhythm with our movement, exhale on exertion, and inhale naturally. It is this posture that enables us to play our best Judo. Sometimes we relax the body in order to relax the mind, and sometimes we reduce our mind's activity to soften the body. The mind and body are one. The Second Life of Judo shows us that being tense is no fun.

"The hard and stiff will be broken, the soft and supple will prevail."
                                                                    – Tao Te Ching

Beginner Judokas often get consumed with pummeling an opponent's arm to secure a power-grip hand position on the opponent's lapel or sleeve. During this obsessive reaching for an upper-hand – while at the same time attempting to break the grip held on their own gi – the beginner becomes susceptible to a counterattack. Awareness of the lower torso, leg movements, foot position, and one's balance become secondary.

The most well-rounded and experienced Judokas adapt and can maneuver from all hand positions. The most resourceful Judokas will even use their hand position as a ploy to draw an opponent's attention away from an intended area of attack. Why is this? Because the most experienced Judokas have years of practice maintaining full-body awareness. This sixth sense gives them the advantage.

Instead of getting involved in the usual sparring for hand position, Mr. B was confident enough in his lightning-quick responses that he would allow his opponents to take his uniform as they pleased. Playing against him was like sitting opposite a world-class speed chess player, who is always two steps ahead of you. Purposely practicing mat work from his back, Mr. B fine-tuned his defensive skills, as he trapped or blocked each and every limb moving towards him. You could not bait him by fighting fire with fire. He always kept his state of equanimity. Non-resistance was his style of Judo play, and it was most efficient, to say the least.

Master Judokas welcome their partner's movements. They are capable of responding with defensive postures, counter-techniques and swift offensive techniques from most body positions. The Master Judoka never forgets that a proper response may even be a Break Fall, when the moment calls for it. Watching the master players, we notice that the most graceful techniques involve a degree of "going along with the flow" of movement initialized by one's practice partner. It is here where we learn the core principles of Judo, which involve non-resistance as a means of self-defense.

Adopting these principles more broadly, we can allow life to act as our practice partner. When we catch a cold, we can listen to our body's requirement for rest and read the book we have had on our night table for months. When we get a bonus, we can take a course on our favorite topic. Or when we feel a strong energy to react in an aggressive manner, we can respond instead by going for a walk in the woods, while taking deep, calming breaths.

Eventually, we see that life's moments are very much like the weather. Allowing the weather to dictate is great practice in responding. Even if you resist the weather, you will learn a valuable lesson soon enough. When it's cold outside, we add another layer of clothing or put on a hat. If we are working outside on a project and a storm comes, we wait for the sky to clear. There is plenty for us to do inside, no problem! What if we had complete trust in life to "move and unfold," exactly as it does? I would imagine we would be filled with great peace, by "trusting life" and responding to its lead.

"Can you trust life to provide you with everything you need to evolve spiritually?"

TEACHING

Mr. B has a Scarf Hold that feels like a death grip from a 20-foot Anaconda. Although he has practiced 40 years to perfect this hold, he rarely uses it. In all my years of practice, I only felt Mr. B's vice-like hold once or twice. Once or twice was enough to understand that at the right angle, with the right leverage, and while using the proven limb positions, even a teenage girl can effectively hold down a much stronger and heavier male Judoka. My teacher didn't feel a need to express this kind of power. Instead, most of the time, he would allow you to roll him over, and he would then go from a top position to a bottom position. His teachings were gentle, and they always infused his students with the heart and the spirit of possibility.

My teacher's style of play was intoxicating to watch, and even more fun to play against. Everyone in the dojo wanted to Randori with him due to his soft style. Kids and adults alike would jump at the chance to test their skills and compete with him. When you were playing with Mr. B, both your Judo and your spirit grew. Think of someone with the wisdom of Yoda, and the speed of Bruce Lee – that is my teacher. Who would be more fun to compete with than that?

My teacher played and taught at such an advanced level that, if he actually felt your technique was executed with proper form and a heartfelt intention, he would allow you to finish and throw or hold him – the key word being "allow." After a perfect break fall, he would pop right up with a look in his eyes, as if he was keeping watch on every Judoka in the room. This look would reveal that Mr. B was just being a gracious teacher. My technique was not sharp enough to catch someone on his level. If I attempted to process what just took place a moment ago, I would find myself being thrown and practicing my own break fall. Mr. B was saying with no words spoken, "Don't think, just allow and respond."

My teacher also had the amazing ability to focus on his opponent during Randori, and still he would somehow know what was going on all the way across the room. At times, he would even guide a student entering a technique on the other side of the mat. "Turn your head, drive through, bend your knees, keep going – you are there," Mr. B would shout, all the while not missing a step with his own partner.

Only a rare smile on my sensei's face would indicate that your technique was strong enough to produce the intended result. Mr. B would then compliment you, if he saw or felt truth in the movement. Only truth in form, truth in sincerity, and truth in effort in every repetition would get you verbal encouragement. The power of his motivating style shone forth to all his students.

"How do you inspire one to learn?
How are you inspired to learn?"

SHRIMP CRAWL

At the beginning of the class, after we go through the bowing ritual, we warm up. We warm up in order to raise our core body temperature and move our body tissues and joints, before we jump into more strenuous activity. The warm up can prevent injury, so it makes sense to do it with the same focus we bring to other parts of class. There is a common warm up movement, called the "Shrimp Crawl." This movement provides the basis for many Judo techniques. Starting on one end of the mat, we first lie on our back. Then, leading with heads, we use only the power in our legs to propel ourselves across the mat. Using our heels as the anchor points in the mat, we push our hips out to the right side, as we rotate and grind our left hips into the mat. At the same time, our right hips rotate upward away from the mat, in a forward direction. The idea is to move straight across the mat in this hip-thrusting and rotating fashion. We are instructed to grab our own judogi at our chest. At no point in the movement do we use our hands.

After we become comfortable with this version of the Shrimp Crawl, we try the more difficult version. Now, we give our hamstrings and abdominals a great workout, as we pull ourselves across the mat, leading with our feet first. Both Shrimp Crawl movements are very useful, because many techniques are applied with our backs on the ground. Both Shrimp Crawl movements allow us to position ourselves just right under our partners, in order to apply a technique at the correct angle, or to ultimately escape from being held down.

You would think that when we are on our back and in the bottom position, we would always want to create distance between our partner's body and our body, to enable an escape. Well, sometimes we do, but other times we want to apply a technique from the very position of being under our practice partner. In the Second Life of Judo, there is no reason to react with panic when our back is on the ground and our opponent is on the top. This position teaches us to welcome all "places," so that when we face a difficult challenge outside the dojo, we find a willingness to welcome all experiences that come. Of course, we may not prefer or desire the experience, but in welcoming all experiences, we find the possibility of transformation. We become more relaxed, therefore able to respond.

MECHANICS, NOT MAGIC

Judo is an art driven by the philosophy of maximum efficiency. For example, imagine two individuals. One individual weighing 175 pounds pushes another individual weighing 130 pounds. The lighter individual has no chance of going strength for strength, of pushing back into the heavier individual to negate his force, so he takes another approach. The lighter individual "allows" the stronger individual to push or pull him in any direction. In this manner, the lighter person essentially becomes similar in shape and resiliency to one of those big exercise balls that have become so popular: The hips act as a fulcrum and the legs like shock absorbers. All the space between the individuals disappears, and the lighter individual dips slightly below the bigger one's waistline. This is how one is literally rolled off one's feet. When the bigger individual is floating on the lighter Judoka's lower back, leg, hip, or foot, it only takes a slight tug on the heavier one's sleeve and a turn of the lighter one's head, in order to literally rotate the bigger person onto his back, before he then hits the mat. This is "maximum efficiency" in action.

Let's use these two individuals again to describe this powerful philosophy, similar in so many ways to the adage "less is more." In this second example, a heavier and stronger individual is about to place his right foot on the ground, as the majority of his weight is coming forward. The lighter individual sweeps that foot a split second before it comes into contact with the mat, thereby re-directing all his weight toward the mat. With the right timing, it becomes quite easy to move 175 pounds, when that weight is already in motion and unstable. It's very similar to the way one only needs to slightly tap a rolling tire in order to change its direction greatly. A proper foot sweep technique has the power to direct the entire body of a much bigger person. Form, commitment, and timing are more important than strength, or even speed. A snap of the Tori's wrist toward the ground with the Uki's lower sleeve in hand – as the sweep is in progress – and the bigger Judoka becomes off balance and is ready to be directed toward the ground, or otherwise set up for another technique.

My last example of maximum efficiency I call the "weak link in the chain." Very strong individuals have proverbial weak links in their chain. We all do; the human body is designed that way. For example, most joints and neck regions are "weak," compared to the more muscular parts of the body. When pressure is applied to these "weak" links, it hurts! Apply the very same pressure to a muscular area like the upper thigh, and your partner will laugh at you. Applying broad pressure to a big muscle group is not using maximum efficiency, but rather is a waste of energy, leaving one easily exhausted. However, apply a small amount of pressure to a specific acupressure point, or a locked joint, and you will see your partner jump or submit. It takes time to learn what areas of the human body are sensitive to pressure and manipulation. The good news is that most people are built more alike than differently, when it comes to nerve sensation and mechanics of joints. Essentially, these "weak links" make strong and weak players more equal.

Experienced Judokas know the human body. They have learned which areas of the body are strong and which are weak. They have learned from years of experience in applying techniques on others and from having techniques applied on them. A Master Judoka may not know anatomy and physiology textbooks as thoroughly as a doctor does, but a Master Judoka still knows anatomy and physiology well enough to understand how to apply a small amount of energy to get a big result. That is maximum efficiency!

When a Judoka applies even a small amount of direct pressure to the carotid artery or the wind pipe for an extended time, there is going to be a result. Blood flow and oxygen to the brain will undoubtedly be affected. This same principle of maximum efficiency can be applied to the manipulation of joints, such as the wrist, elbow, shoulder, or ankle. Joints themselves are considered weak, because they connect points between two or more bones, and are therefore stabilized by ligaments. Joints are designed to have a certain (limited) range of motion, and they tend to lock at a specific point in their range of motion. A small amount of pressure goes a long way when it comes to locking joints. There is just very little flexibility or muscle strength available to unlock joints, once they are beyond a certain range of motion. This is true for the joints of even the biggest and strongest individuals. For example, notice that your knee joint is essentially designed to bend one way, and only one way. Apply pressure to the knee joint in the few directions that it is not designed to move, and it hurts!

Weak links come in many other forms. It may only be after a lighter and weaker Judoka has been thrown around before he notices that his partner's endurance and cardiovascular condition is decreasing greatly. The lighter Judoka's muscles continue to receive blood and oxygen, and whatever else they need in order to strongly contract. The lighter Judoka continues to feel "light on his feet." The heavier Judoka, on the other hand, is not doing so well. He is exhausted. He is breathing heavy. He can't keep his arms up or maintain his Jigo-Hontai (see definition). The Judoka that started off strong becomes sloppy, slower, and usually drops his guard, creating opportunities for the lighter Judoka to follow through with techniques and score points. Now, the lighter Judoka gets a chance to enjoy the benefit of his endurance work. Judokas of all shapes, sizes, conditioning and strength are free to use the principles of maximum efficiency to improve their Judo. Some may want to increase speed, strength, or cardiovascular stamina and endurance. And, some may want to improve their mat work form or their standing techniques. In all these areas, the maximum efficiency principle is applicable.

Versions of maximum efficiency are practically endless. This is what makes Judo so much fun; it's a never-ending dance with your partner's energy. As you are beginning to see, the art involves so much more than brute strength.

When one relies only on a weight or strength advantage, then one's timing, conditioning, form, and application of the maximum efficiency philosophy all become secondary, and his Judo ultimately suffers.

"How can you apply the principle of maximum efficiency today?"

NOT GOOD OR BAD

An important message was being sent when we played Judo with my teacher. He was showing us that being thrown is just as much a part of the sport as being the thrower. Being in a challenging spot is just as much a part of the sport, and just as much a part of life, as being in a comfortable spot. Everything that takes place on the mat or off is an experience that holds value. Mr. B made it very clear that there is value in being thrown, just as there is value in throwing your partner. When we get thrown, we become better "fallers." As we are thrown, for example, we learn the importance of slightly tucking our chin into our chest to protect our head. And, as we get thrown repeatedly, we likely feel a slight variation, or interpretation, of a technique by our opponent; a variation that we haven't necessarily felt before. Therefore, we more instinctively know how to defend against those variations the next time.

Whether we are on one or the other side of Kesa-gatame (see definition), we learn. When we are being held down, we learn how to create distance between the holder and our own body, so that we can practice maneuvering with greater mobility and escape. When we are holding down another, we learn to keep our head down, so that it doesn't get hooked by our partner's leg. Both positions hold great value, and we become more efficient players, having been on both sides many times.

Is this not the ebb and flow of life? Some days it rains; some days it's sunny. Is this not the ebb and flow of Judo Play? Some days we are on top; some days we are on the bottom. What if we said, "No problem!"

Mr. B was very clear about applying the lesson we learn outside the dojo walls; Everything We Experience Holds Value. The Second Life of Judo doesn't categorize one experience as bad, and another as good. The Second Life of Judo expresses all experiences as one life to be lived, one arrow that has been released from its bow and now flies into a great mystery.

"The good may become bad, the bad may become good.
Maybe there is no such thing as either?"

BALANCE

During competitive practice, we are taught not to shift all our body weight onto one leg. If that weight-bearing limb is attacked, we are susceptible to being thrown. With one's weight more evenly distributed throughout the surface of the mat (right, left, front, back, light and heavy), it enables us to instantly switch power back and forth between legs. Not only does the balance produce a better defense, it enables us to score points with speedy and efficient counter-techniques, made in response to our partner's initial attack. Judo is an ongoing practice of adjustment and response.

"Live with Balance" and "Balance in Life" are adages instructing us not to cling too much to any one thing. When we dig our roots of attachment too deep into one place, we are setting ourselves up for a fall. This is not much different than planting one leg holding our entire weight in front of our partner. Balance in life and balance in the dojo is being light on our feet, and staying capable of adjusting and responding in the moment. Experienced Judokas play Judo this way.

If you practice Judo long enough, you can feel the growth and decline in each one of your movements. Some techniques in Judo grow and decline more quickly – like a breaking wave appears to us when we are sitting on a beach. Some techniques in Judo mature more slowly. They appear to have a more mountainous quality and hold position for a longer period of time.

Judo further teaches us to enjoy both the growth and decline stages of life, of class and of technique. It teaches us to notice our center of gravity, and watch out for what attempts to pull or push us off balance. When we hold a fixed grip on the judogi, or dig a foot position deep into the mat, we become unbalanced. As we become more experienced in Judo, we move fluidly through stages of growth and decline without any resistance when changing from one position to another.

The ego will tell us that we need to change something externally to find peace internally. The ego will beg us to chase after the next prize guaranteeing our satisfaction and lasting happiness once attained. In the Second Life of Judo, we do not get pushed or pulled around by the ego's directives anymore. This steady grounded place is a place of balance.

It is said that the Judokas' balance depends upon their inner state of being. What pulls you off balance? Can you feel the difference between reacting and responding?

NO MIND

We can spend a lifetime experimenting with all the dynamics that come together to create a beautiful and effortless technique. The Second Life of Judo encourages us to explore the factors that make one technique beautiful rather than learning ten techniques adequately. Going deeply into one thing, instead of going shallowly into many, will take us far in the dojo, and in life.

Do we turn our head and follow through in one fluid motion? Do we enter into the technique from an unusual distance? Do we release our grip on our opponent's sleeve too early? Do we pull our opponent off-balance enough? Do we thrust our hip out far enough? Do we bend our knees, to use the lifting power in our legs? Do we hesitate because we are afraid of being countered, or do we work to finish our technique, and continue to complete the technique, even when we are initially stopped? Go deep and all the answers will be lived!

There is a technique in Judo called the Rear Sacrifice Throw. In Japanese it's called Tomoe Nage, which translates as the Circular Throw. This particular technique has a deep significance. It is a classic example of "dying while still alive." There is no doing a Circular Throw half-heartedly. We burn ourselves up completely in the attempt. This "dying" into the technique is the only way it manifests as beautiful art.

If we hesitate, look back, over-think, or don't commit 100 percent to the technique, the technique will fall short. Even when we give our all to this technique, we are very exposed and vulnerable to being held down by our opponent if one part of the whole falters. This is why it's a true Sacrifice Technique in every sense of the word.

In order to complete this throw, the Tori is literally sacrificing his body position. The Tori's back is on or close to the mat, and the Uki is hovering over the Tori. If the Tori's foot misses its mark – the lower abdominal region of the Uki – or if Uki blocks the technique, or if there is the slightest telegraphing or hesitation on the Tori's part, then most likely the technique will fall apart, and the Tori will be held down.

Learning from past experiences – then having the focus to let it all go – is the "edge" we walk on during sacrifice techniques. A Judoka has to have the courage to enter into a sacrifice technique many times before the result feels just right. A true sacrifice thrusts us into the moment. We instantly become present. All we have are the few seconds in the now, as we give ourselves up to the technique. The technique, our body, and the moment become one and the same. This is the meaning of the common spiritual art phrase "no mind" or "empty mind." When we experience "empty mind" during a technique, it is indeed special. But please, don't chase after the "empty mind" experience; just continue to practice hard, and it comes in its own time.

A spiritual art gives us the practice and experience of being in the now. It is a wonderful gift that is offered. How many of us are willing to experience life "dying while still alive?" Is the day filled with obsessing about the past or future expectations, believing the "maybe I should" or "maybe I shouldn't have" conversation in our heads? When we drop the weight of the past and the future from our shoulders, we feel so much better, no matter how things work out.

A Judoka of many years experience knows that the greatest techniques are performed with little or no physical strength. It's called "flow." The energy to perform a grand technique is already there in the present. Actually, it's provided by the moment. Scoring on your experienced partner with an effortless technique is how you know your Judo is sharp. Right there, is where the flesh is filled with spirit.

> *What did the Yogi Zen Master say to the Hotdog Street Vendor?*
> *"Make me ONE with everything."*
> *— Zen Humor*

PARTICIPATION

Mr. B's message has always been, "to participate is the reward." A child that is acting out is simply told to sit on the edge of the mat and watch. Doing something extremely fun at the right time, like having the class climb up and over a huge crash pad, adds an extra incentive for a child who is sitting out to cooperate. Soon, that child is willing to give up individual antics for a chance to jump back in and work with the group for the best interest of the group.

It was fascinating to watch my teacher establish rules and boundaries with children and adults alike. Being head of a dojo requires giving and receiving great respect from all who walk through the door. That includes overly possessive parents as well as pumped-up Harley Davidson dudes. There is a place called "center," in which respect is naturally given and received. Where or what is the center? It's a handshake, or greeting someone with a smile. It is taking time to find out how someone is doing; remaining calm in the face of strong opinions; not getting dragged here or there, by being caught up in one's own opinions. And certainly, it is also a place where abuse is not tolerated.

On rare occasions, an adult student might also act childishly and test the code of respect and sportsmanship of the art. At these times, Mr. B's remedy was simple. Mr. B would then hand-pick the next four or five opponents for this ornery adult. Forty minutes of straight Randori with advanced and conditioned students was enough to drain hostile energy out of any rebellious student. One becomes very humble, after being thrown to the ground and held down repeatedly for 40 minutes. Another humbling alternative would come when this once-edgy adult had to ask permission to rest. It was easy to see: what served the class also served the individual. Looking back, I see that my teacher's actions were indeed kind, and adults and children alike would benefit by understanding the boundaries set forth by the sensei. Even within such a controlled setting, there is always "space" allowed for one's individuality to shine forth. Every Judoka has his or her own unique style of play.

Anyone who showed up to class with no uniform in hand was always greeted with a smile, and an "OK" to come on in. Mr. B would always find a way to make that person feel welcome. Most who stepped through the dojo door for the very first time would feel intimidated at first. Some would come for stress-reduction, some for conditioning and weight loss, some to learn self defense, some to prove something. But none of this mattered because, in the big picture, what they first experienced was kindness and compassion.

I remember how Mr. B would ask the most senior student to take over the class as he would walk over to talk to a new observer. Mr. B would be very insightful and non-intimidating in this process. He would tell us that some people just want the experience of watching class to see what is offered. In these cases, a simple and friendly introduction is best. As Judokas, we must allow the observer to experience what they have come for. With more eager observers, it was common to hear Mr. B. say, "Feel free to join us – I have extra Judogis in the locker room."

Mr. B seemed to have limitless energy to devote time and attention to all beginners, as well as to his advanced students. He had a knack for knowing who he didn't get a chance to work with one-on-one, even in a class of 20 students. If a situation arose that called for him to give a lot of time to one particular student, he would gladly do so. Even at the end of an extended class, he would nonchalantly address the one or two students that he was not able to practice with and let them know he would get to them during the next class. And he would always live up to his word. Mr. B also made it a habit to rotate partners during Uchikomi (see definition), just as he did during the rest of the class. For Mr. B, there was no substitute for being "hands on" with his students, in order to know if their technique was improving.

Seeing Mr. B welcome a newcomer was special. In his own way, his welcoming was saying, "I accept you just as you are; the class accepts you just as you are; the dojo accepts you just as you are; and you will learn to accept yourself just as you are." It is in this field of acceptance that we become present, and learn to practice Judo as a Spiritual Art.

BREAK FALLS

Walking into a Judo class for the first time may be a rude awakening for many. Arriving with visions of grandeur of throwing other people around the dojo is a fantasy. Before one even gets a chance to grab hold of a single lapel, the newcomer will be whisked away to a remote corner of the mat to practice Break Falls for a good half an hour. Back Falls, Side Falls, Front Falls and Judo Rolls are the majority of a beginner's initiation to the sport. There is even a running joke among experienced practitioners: "Let's see if he or she makes it through the first few months of Break Falls." Often muscular guys come into the dojo, full of piss and vinegar, looking to put a whooping on folks. But instead, they are told to practice Break Falls before they can even touch another human being. Look over at these new students after just 20 minutes, and you will see that they are deflated, frustrated and tired.

The coordination and timing of a proper Break Fall technique or Judo Roll will test even the most committed beginner. Learning how to fall is arduous, but essential. It is the repetition which enables our limbs and breathing to flow in sync without any thought involved. We can't proceed without first achieving a certain level of form and confidence in falling. A dojo would be sure to have no students if the sensei allowed beginners to jump right into competitive practice without attaining proper falling skills. Injuries would run rampant. Even after a couple months of practicing Break Falls, it is not uncommon for a beginning student to bounce their head off the mat or land awkwardly during a fall. Only after many months of falling, will an individual have the sufficient full-body awareness to land with ease after being thrown.

Let's face it, falling hard to the ground and getting the wind knocked out of you (which is not uncommon for a beginner) is not as much fun as punching stationary pads, kicking a practice dummy, or learning how to defend against a mock attack from a mugger with a wooden knife. It's no secret that Judo has seen a great decline in popularity over the last few decades. It takes a very dedicated and humble individual to get through the first couple of years of being thrown frequently. Hitting the mat with more and more ease becomes the first real sign of improvement and represents the first step on the journey of the "Gentle Way."

In the Second Life of Judo, we breathe through the many metaphorical Break Falls of the aging process. As we age, our body changes. We inhabit these changes, and our willingness continually props us back up. We repeat this process for as long as possible. If we are lucky enough to live to 80, 90, or 100, we still consider ourselves just elderly beginners. This is how we are inspired to continue. We have the First Life of Judo to thank for the basic teachings in falling, rolling gently, and then finding our feet back under us.

RITUALS

Judokas tap the mat or anywhere accessible on their opponent's body to signal that they surrender. The amount of acceptance and humility that comes along with "tapping" is staggering. The moment we tap, we find it is surprisingly very easy. No ego lives inside this moment, no ego breathes inside this action. When we surrender, there is no resistance. It is freeing and feels like a wonderful release, despite what one may think. Try it sometime. The threat is over. We see it never really existed in the first place! Surrender is not a gesture of weakness. In fact, surrender is one of the most powerful forms of acceptance and signs of inner strength. This moment of surrender teaches us to live life with a gentle heart, for we all face challenging times sooner or later. We carry the Judo of surrender outside the dojo into the larger practice ground of life.

You may have heard the guttural vocal sounds that the martial artist makes when expressing exertion. The kiai (shout) is made when an individual wants to dig down deep into his gut for the additional energy needed to complete an action. The kiai originates from the lower abdominals, a place where we cultivate courage. "That took a lot of guts" and "he or she has some set of balls" are statements related to this region. On a more practical level, this region is our center of gravity. There is a place where the external exercise (technique) meets the internal energetic expression (kiai). The union between the external movements and the internal expression will produce our greatest power and fluidity.

A martial artist knows through experience that the kiai is a source of power in and of itself. When technique and the kiai are one, it is said that "The Web of Sound and Movement Unite Earth and Heaven" – a metaphor for expressing how physical and spiritual power come together to produce something very sacred. When we are young and fit, the muscle carries the weight. In the Second Life of Judo we know that our spiritual strength carries us when we are old and frail.

Bowing is an age-old ritual of the martial arts. We bow to each other to show respect. We respect that our fellow man and woman have shown up to practice, and it is this very willingness that is honored with the bow. The bow is a gesture that falls somewhere between a handshake and a hug. The bow also has a more subtle meaning. Notice the body language of a bow: Our legs remain strong and rooted, and our upper body is slightly lowered. The bow shows strength within humility. In a proper bow, our gaze becomes small and aims low, showing humility to our adversary. When we bow to our partner, we are certainly not in a position to defend ourselves; therefore, it's the ultimate demonstration of trust. We trust that our opponents have the character within themselves not to attack when we are at an unfair advantage. They trust us equally with their bows.

Bowing to the head instructor before stepping onto the mat is a call for each Judoka to consciously rise up. It has little to do with rising up to a physical challenge. Rather, the call is to show gratitude for being able to participate and to share the knowledge that this very moment will never come again. With this awareness, class can only be good practice, even if we experience a day of poor technique or low energy.

The "Attention Bow" is announced at the beginning of class. This sacred announcement cuts to the heart of our intention. We practice being 100% where we are. It's not 90% here practicing technique, and 10% over there thinking about our boyfriend or girlfriend. The spiritual question in the Second Life of Judo is this: Do we have the courage to live fully in each moment, as if it could be our last?

The fashion in which our uniform is folded and cared for is a reflection of everything that we do, and it shows how far we have progressed in the art as a lifestyle. We care for the fibers of the judogi, as if they made up another layer of our very skin. There is a specific way of folding the gi after it is cleaned and dry. As we fold the judogi and breathe, we are reminded that we are present and the act becomes a ritual. If we take the time to properly care for our uniform, then we have the awareness to take the time to properly care for our body. If we show up to the dojo with a clean uniform, we show up to the dojo with a clean conscience. When we show up with a neatly folded uniform, we show up with our affairs in order.

The day we grab our judogi unfolded and run out of the house is the same day we forget to smile, walk in the park, listen to a friend, or focus on how we truly wish to live the life our heart talks about. Wearing the judogi indicates that we are "here," inside the gi, inside the dojo, and ready to practice.

"How we do anything is how we do everything."
– Cheri Huber

FINISHING

As we mature into the Second Life of Judo, our responsibilities become clear. We make sure that the beginner has correct form, and if we can make adjustments to his or her technique, we do so. We find that "middle ground" place between instructing and allowing – a place of balance between correction and encouragement. Advanced students demonstrate by being living examples of Judokas, with relaxed central nervous systems, proving that their technique is safe and effective.

Experienced Judokas encourage beginners to "finish" a technique once it is started. Often, beginners do not want to fully commit to an offensive movement, for fear of being countered. And so, they "back out" of their intended technique, or hesitate. Completing a movement trains beginners to drop the habit of playing it safe – a habit that will not serve them in the dojo or in life. Training to finish reassures us over and over again that there are no mistakes to be made, just experiences to be lived.

A complete technique is really a lot of minor details strung together, culminating in one fluid movement. Foundational movements of Judo, such as

Kuzushi (see definition), foot entry, body spacing, and lifting and turning at proper angles are so important because these movements are applicable for as long as we continue the art. If just one minor detail falters, the technique may still be pulled off, but it will not be effortless, graceful and beautiful. Advanced students working with beginners have creative insights for infusing "fun" into the practice experience.

"With Beginner's Mind, the advanced becomes the student and the student becomes the advanced."

Writing a book sometimes takes years of commitment. After reading a great book, a first-time author may easily doubt that his book will compare. These are the same doubting voices that talk to us during our first few months in the dojo, when we see advanced Judokas with 25 years of experience. There is nothing left to do but tighten our obi and turn our attention to that which will provide inspiration and encouragement. The voices of self-doubt and comparison want nothing good for us. They just want to get us to quit! We can recognize these voices for what they are, and choose to laugh and practice. Channeling the wise-loving mentor that wants the best for us as we work, practice, play, write, study, or do anything is how we keep going and finish. We finish when we are having fun.

"If one enters the Dojo powered by muscle and air alone, one's technique will fall short."

THE DOJO:
A SPIRITUAL DESIGN

THE MAT SPACE

The dojo is a sacred place. It is literally a training ground where the physical body and the spirit meet. The mat is for the Judoka what the canvas is for the ink artist. It is a place where we learn to have respect for our own body, and therefore, we have respect for the bodies of our fellow men and women.

It is easy to see that "empty space" is regarded as beautiful in the dojo. Everything is designed to flow around the practice area and highlight the mat. If you want to understand the concept of Feng Shui (see definition), go to a dojo. From your very entrance, it is easy to feel the flow of energy that circulates and pulls you toward the mat.

The open space always makes the simple character and history of a brick wall or an old hardwood floor look beautiful. Windows are kept crystal-clean, to allow the rays of natural light to shine through. Air from outside is circulated through the lungs and through the dojo, when weather permits. Walls are never overly adorned – a single item may be hanging – for they remind us to remain grateful to the culture that designed this special practice. Outside the dojo, wind chimes whisper the sounds of simplicity.

A locker room is necessary to store possessions like cell phones, watches, and jewelry neatly out of sight. Everyday belongings are put aside for the duration of class. We rediscover that we can detach ourselves, respond well without our possessions, and then enjoy them again after class with renewed appreciation.

The dojo says to us that this spiritual practice ground reinforces everything we do. We are grateful for a place to practice, just as we are grateful for a roof over our heads at night. The dojo can always be the very earth beneath our feet. It is said, that even the spectator becomes a participant, when one practices the principles of martial arts. Caring for ourselves and for the people and things surrounding us is practicing the ultimate principle of spiritual arts. We certainly do not need to step foot on the mat, or even be inside a traditional arena, such as a Dojo or Zendo, to care for ourselves and our surroundings.

"Mr. B. spoke of the mat as the great equilizer. The one place where the lawyer and the garbageman are equals."

PICTURE PERFECT

More often than not, you will notice a single piece of art surrounded by a simple wood frame hanging in the locker room. At first you may disregard the picture, but like a magnetic force it will soon draw your attention. For the picture is of an elderly man or an elderly woman sitting very still on a mountainside. Their age symbolizes wisdom. Their eyelids are lightly closed, and their teapot will be at their side. Their bodies will be well-wrapped in layers of cloth, to convey the message of comfort within a meditative state. Their retreat in the middle distance, with its Torii Gate Entrance, blends into the peaks and valleys of a mountain range, and the highs and lows of the receding horizon embody Yin and Yang characteristics. Also, a perfect 'V' formation of geese soars through the skyline, to demonstrate movement within stillness. And deep in the valley below, there is a running creek, which signifies impermanence. In this way, the dojo is filled with subtle inspiration connecting us with Nature.

In the well-known image of the Zen monastery, even activities related to cleaning the body inside the dojo are conducted with great order and simplicity. In the shower stall area, one will find a small amount of cedar wood and stone, to pay homage to the Onsen (see definition), which, after centuries, still remains the natural place where people bathe in Japan.

THE OFFICE

The dojo's office is usually small in size, so that more room may be devoted for mat space. The flowing ink stone calligraphy that adorns the walls behind the Sensei's desk pays tribute to a code of conduct known as "Way of the Warrior." This artwork is designed to convey the code of conduct that needs to be lived inside the dojo, one which includes a deep respect for our fellow man or woman Judoka. More often than not, the desk and chairs are worn and aged, signifying comfort and wisdom. You will always be able to find instructional books, guides, and Master Teacher tapes collected on the shelves. Photo albums of participants from over the years are also kept in the sensei's office.

A trophy shelf is also a common sight in the office. My instructor always made a point to note that the trophy itself was not important, but knowing that one's Judo has improved is worth something. Mr. B said that one does not have to win a trophy to know one's Judo has improved. This is why the dojo team trophy sits front and center. It signifies a cohesive group's hard work on timing, leverage, favorite techniques, stamina, counters, combinations, and most of all, character. For my instructor, a winning trophy from any student was symbolic of a group effort. Our dojo always played just a little harder for Mr. B, precisely because he never asked us to.

When looking around, don't be surprised if you notice nothing but three judogis hanging neatly in the office closet. These are the few material possessions that matter most to the sensei. Even for the sensei, the judogi (or gi) is an ever-present reminder of his or her responsibility to the art. The gi is the umbilical cord, which allows the art to come to life. Putting on the gi is where the rubber meets the road. It is like jumping on a horse, or diving into the deep end of a pool. There is no "half way." It's in or out, on or off the mat. When we are in our gi, we are riding, or treading water, or practicing the "Gentle Way." *Doing* is how we learn.

THE GREAT EQUALIZER

My teacher considered his dojo as his home, and all his students were welcomed as family. He was the ultimate host, providing a complete martial art experience. Intense practice lived within an easy-going atmosphere. Laughter always seemed to balance out the teaching of precise details. Only our mental conditioning tells us that "intense" and "easy-going," or "demanding" and "fun," can't co-exist. Mr. B's gymnastic background never strayed from the old school roots of his traditional 7th-degree Japanese Teacher. Sticking a landing off a mini-trampoline for warm-ups soon turned into polished Kodokan Judo (see definition). Judo practice remained a sacred art, an exercise and a privilege of self-expression, regardless of one's rank, skill level, or position in society. Mr. B spoke of the practice mat as the Great Equalizer. He explained that it is the one place where the lawyer and the garbageman are equals. As soon as you step onto the mat – man or woman, old or young, big or small – you are equals.

"Spirit beats body 10 out of 10 times"

"*What comes* *from the heart* *goes straight* **to the heart.**"
— *Artist Saying*

PIERCING THE EGO

WAY OF THE WOUND

When an irritant slips into the shell of an oyster, its natural response is to protect its inner core by secreting a substance called nacre. Strangely enough, it is also the nacre that makes the beautiful pearl. In fact, without the presence of the irritant, no pearl would be made. Life itself provides irritants all the time. If we resist "what is," we suffer. But if we *accept* what is, we have just taken the first steps on the path to freedom. When an irritant is present in our lives, the question becomes: What expectations do I have of myself right now? What set of standards do I have to meet? Can I live through the change? Can I allow change to live through me?

When one's physical capabilities are taken away, it pierces the ego and humbles a person very quickly. In a split second, my life changed from knowing and successfully pursuing my dreams, to seemingly knowing nothing. The experience felt like death, because it was indeed a kind of death – a death of the ego.

At first, I rebelled against my chronic nerve injury every step of the way, and further thought that, in some delusional way, resisting "what is" was being strong. I had one depressive emotional reaction after another while my ego held the reigns, which only made me more and more miserable. I pushed along with a "mind-over-matter" philosophy, challenging myself to overcome or outwit life's uncertainties, which naturally led to more pain and suffering. It was an exhausting five years! The abusive relationship that "I" maintained had to stop; and thank goodness it did.

The 1st place medal that I received for winning The Garden State Games was now meaningless. My 15-year career as a Personal Trainer, my black belt, my nutrition degree from the University of Delaware, and my Yoga Instructor Certification all became useless to me. There was no salvation now in any of those accomplishments. My identity was torn apart in a split second, just as easily as a Samurai Sword cuts through rice paper.

I couldn't rely on the past or the future to reveal the truth. I couldn't escape the pain – and believe me, I did my best to do just that. Nothing would give me the relief that I was looking for. I was left with no choice but to feel everything completely within my body (both the physical pain and the resistance of my ego to accept the situation).

It takes a tremendous amount of courage to live in a spiritual state of non-resistance to life's many hardships. When we say "Yes" to "what is," we are free to respond. When we respond, we are no longer victims. This is "spiritual freedom." When we are no longer pushed around by thoughts of "could have, would have, or should have," we are free. Forget about rewinding the tape of life, or hitting the fast forward button. Instead, use everything in your life, past and present, as raw ingredients to cook a precious meal. In fact, suffering and difficulty are the raw ingredients necessary for spiritual transformation. It's from these raw ingredients that the spirit of willingness emerges. I soon realized: Life's irritants often start out as our enemies. But then they transform into challenges, and lastly, become gifts. The transformation that results from going through the difficult situation is the blessing.

Just like when we learn Judo and learn how to relax when we are about to be thrown, spiritual practice is ingested much in the same way – little by little, over and over, day in and day out, moment by moment – usually with many stumbles along the way. It's how we overcome both mind and muscle. When we find ourselves calm, compassionate and grateful, while being in a situation that others may consider a tragedy, we know something magical has occurred. We all have what it takes to flush the suffering from our blood, and access the inner pearl of wisdom and peace for all of life.

TRUE PRACTICE

I have a vivid memory of my teacher's Black Belt: It was so worn, that it had turned grey. Only a few strands of black fabric still remained within the fabric of the belt. Obviously, the weathering of his belt signified the countless hours he had spent on the practice mat. Whether it was teaching six-year-old kids, or working with nationally ranked competitors, his belt and his body were subject to the wear and tear of the sport. I know that over Mr. B's lifetime, a few of his Black Belts had been worn down even more. To this day, I can still imagine how thousands of gripping hands would soften a judogi, such as the one he wore.

Hard work and sacrifice for the things we are passionate about is part of the spiritual path. Many years ago I fell in love with yoga. I really don't remember exactly when I first felt this interest, but the practice offered everything I was looking for. It was physical, meditative, non-violent, and all about the spiritual aspects of breathing. That summer, I traveled to an ashram found high in the mountains of Colorado. I immersed myself in everything yoga. Hours of meditation followed hours of Asana practice, followed by breathing exercise, followed by vegetarian meals, followed by cleaning dishes, followed by more meditation. I enjoyed every minute of it, although I missed my wife and family back home.

I came down from the mountain with a plan to teach yoga. But, as is often said, I had a plan and God was laughing. It was only months later that I found myself in great pain due to a nerve injury. Instead of leading a group of others through an exhilarating practice, I was home on the couch taking pain killers.

It was so hard for me to even watch my wife practice her yoga, knowing that I couldn't participate. I was compelled to leave her vicinity when she practiced. That difficult time taught me to stop believing there is an "alternative to what is." Once I stopped that belief, I got on with the business of living in the now – of living the one and only life that is. A transformation started to occur. The balance of the scale was slowly shifting from resistance to acceptance.

After some agonizing but transformational years, I found myself in my room doing yoga again. This yoga practice was not made up of postures, such as hand stands and side planks. Instead, it was a yoga practice of deep, slow, expansive breathing. That's it, just breathing. Nonetheless, this practice became sacred time. I was experiencing more and more freedom, even as my condition baffled me. My yoga practice became more of an art of "not doing" than "having to do." Then, I graduated to 20 minutes of a more active routine consisting of a few neck rolls, facial exercises, breathing, and meditation. My yoga practice then evolved into slow, steady hip rolls, acupressure applied to the bottom of my feet, and self-massage given to my lower back, with a few gentle shoulder shrugs and a few restorative poses. All these movements had a releasing quality to them. I was releasing any involuntary contraction of my muscles. I watched the power of the breath dictate movements of my body. With each natural exhale I found musculature of my lower back and even my jaw, releasing tension little by little.

I was doing a true practice for the very first time. It didn't consist of advanced postures or keeping up with the person on the mat next to me. My practice consisted of doing what *I* could, and being at peace with that. I knew it was a true practice the moment I was able to be with my wife as she did her practice, and I was not compelled to leave the room. Watching her was not painful. That itch of resentment was gone. I was happy for her, knowing her yoga was important for her peace of mind, and for an aligned physical body. I knew more about yoga practice than ever before, and I was grateful for the lesson life had provided. My intention all along – from the very first time that I felt a tug – was to know the core teaching of yoga. And it was revealed to me in time. This lesson was worth all the heartbreak.

> *"If you can't feel the pain, you can't feel the joy."*
> *– Warrior saying*

> *"What are you grateful for? How do you celebrate life?"*

CARE FOR THE BODY

Being in good physical condition enables us to plant seeds in our garden, walk the dog up hills and help our partner carry the groceries. We must take care of the body, or how else will we carry the body through life? Caring for the body is appreciating the very gift of life. Is your body thanking you for treating it the way you do?

In the Second Life of Judo, we remain very grateful for our life and for our body, just the way it is; and this is the place we start from over and over again. Knowing how to take care of ourselves is a wisdom that we attain in the Second Life of Judo. Intuitively, we know that taking care of ourselves includes: being in nature, hugging a pet, simplifying our schedules, getting quality hours of sleep, enjoying a hobby, closing our eyes in silence, focusing on our breath and laughing with our kids. All of these activities are centering and self-caring.

Do you give your body what it requires, such as gentle exercise, adequate rest, clean water, and nutritious food? Or do you treat your body as your slave, holding it to standards that it must live up to? And, if it doesn't meet your level of expectation, do you force it to comply? Sure, we can care for the body, and all the while remember we are eventually letting go of its form. When we take care of ourselves, we see an improvement in the quality of our life, no matter how long our life might be. Let this be your encouragement and seed of motivation. Soon, our legs won't carry us anymore, our fingers won't grip for us anymore, and our ears won't hear for us anymore. But our heart will carry us through! Let's make the best of our time.

Make your own "self-care" list. Don't be talked into taking the list down off the refrigerator. Watch how your ego tells you that "you know" the list by now and therefore do not need to be reminded every day. Notice how voices of self-hate tell you that the list is just another stressful "thing" in your life to attend to. Be aware of how conditioning talks you into having to do everything on the list and then tells you that ten minutes of self-care is probably not worth it, so you may as well postpone it. Listen to the "encourager," instead, who allows you to pick one thing on the list and apply yourself to that one thing. Stay in touch with the encouraging voice, and be the one who always treats yourself well, no matter what.

The activities on your list come with "do-it-yourself" instructions. No one can do these tasks for you. The personal trainer, the life coach, or the spiritual guide can point the way, but they can't make it happen for you. It starts and ends with your own willingness.

Today, walk five minutes longer than you "think" you can. Tomorrow, walk ten minutes less than you "usually" do. This way you can see who is really in charge of walking. Walking can be anything.

EFFORTLESS EFFORT

I have a friend who runs ultra-marathons, which often consist of covering a distance of over 100 miles in 40 hours or less. My friend has finished several of these marathons, while, at the same time, dealing with extreme weather, dangerous elevations and rocky terrain. Blisters, vomiting, nausea, and ten-minute cat naps are just part of the grueling experience. You can imagine the training and preparation that my friend endures to be able to accomplish this feat. His body and his mind are extremely focused and hardy, by the time he enters a race.

My friend is successful at completing ultras, because he commits to an intense physical conditioning program and has a terrific ability to respond moment by moment to whatever may come. He welcomes all experiences. He knows that dealing with the unforeseen and the uncontrollable is a natural part of these very long and taxing competitions. Responding mindfully to the uncontrollable is a huge part of ultra-marathon running, and a huge part of awareness practice as well. Training ourselves to respond to the uncertainty, instability, and inconsistency of life is worthwhile conditioning. I often tell my friend that his marathons are a wonderful practice for life and that he is training as a "Zen Monk." For him, the running trail is his monastery.

After Mr. B retired from teaching Judo, he told me that he wishes everyone would be so lucky to find a sacred practice ground for the second half of life. He expressed that what takes place on the farm is similar to what took place in the dojo. Judo for him now is fine-tuning the art of caring for the horses and the land. Mr. B is very fortunate to be so passionate about the environment of his Second Life of Judo.

"Right now is your best opportunity to practice kindness.
What is your Monastery?"

THE MANTRA

In 2000, I was lucky enough to meet a woman, whom to this day, I consider my spiritual teacher. Mr. B taught me with movement and action inside a dojo, and this woman, whom I will call "Mrs. B" taught me outside the dojo with stillness. For over ten years now, she has been a beyond-influential source of wisdom and compassion for me. This magnificent woman has a deep trust in life. When in her presence, the whole room is filled with an energy that seems to travel with you for a short time after you leave her.

I remember exactly where I was, the exact sequence of words that were spoken and the "lightning-in-a-bottle feeling" that came over me when this spiritual teacher gave me a three-word mantra. This three-word mantra summed up our ten years of work together and the 40 years of work to come. My mantra is of no importance to you. If I were to write this mantra for you, the words would just be letters on a page. If I were to speak this mantra to you, the sounds would be empty dialogue that you have already heard from other spiritual teachers.

A mantra is a word or group of words that are usually repeated during prayer, or before or after meditation and yoga practice. Mantras can come in handy anytime during the day. Mantras can be silently repeated when a friend is dying, when the phone at work is ringing off the hook, or when you are in the shower. Some actually prefer chanting their mantra while holding Mala beads. In any case, mantras neither need to be chanted, counted, nor contain a certain amount of words. The mantra certainly doesn't need to be fortified by accompanying music, dancing, or incense. The only thing words need in order to be a mantra, is that you feel their power deep inside your soul, causing a peaceful shift. That's it!

A mantra is like the air we breathe, or the body itself: they are given to us without our having to do a thing. Your mantra may have already been given to you. You don't need to travel to India to have a spiritual teacher, and you certainly don't need a spiritual teacher to receive a mantra. A mantra may come from a bum on the street, your bible, a Bodhisattva in disguise, from the internet, or from your seven-year-old niece. After ten years of reading, studying, and memorizing a 900- page book, you may suddenly simply notice the phrase written on the bookmark that you have been using all those years. That phrase strikes something deep within your soul that is freeing; that is how the mantra appears.

Most of us get up in the morning and simply put on pants, without being aware of the arm, leg, and lower back movements this act involves. Then one morning, we become aware of "how" we put our pants on. The mantra may be right in front of you and appears when you see through a new pair of eyes. The words themselves may not be new, but you will hear them with new ears. When I heard the phrase spoken by my spiritual teacher, it was like I was exiting a dense forest after many years of wandering. It was like taking one step beyond the tree line into an open field under the light and warmth of the sun. It was enlightening. There certainly will be more woods to walk through, but now I have more motivation to keep walking no matter where I may be, because I have met peace in the moment. It is now your time to discover the peace that is in this moment, and within you.

GROUNDLESSNESS

Ultimately, the deepest teachings of Judo relate to "groundlessness." Through balancing our body, we get a better understanding of what it means to have no ground underneath our feet. Sometimes one foot is on the ground, sometimes both feet are on the ground, and sometimes no part of our body is touching ground. As we practice the art of Judo, we experience the continuum between being grounded and groundlessness. This makes Judo one of the great teachers of how to flow with change. The more we practice, the better we get at going with the flow of life and the flow of Judo. The more we practice, the more it becomes apparent that life moves us.

No matter how hard we dig our feet into the mat, or how much we squat down to lower our center of gravity, if we practice long enough, there will always be a time when we become groundless. If we live long enough, the very same occurs outside the dojo. We may prefer precise answers to our questions, but there comes the time when we just don't know any answers. Although we may prefer security, we are often forced to live on shaky ground.

"Spiritual arts give us practice in accepting groundlessness."

A recurring theme in all the spiritual arts is "a welcoming of everything." The things that appear the most challenging become our brightest teachings, when we stop pushing them away. The moment we think we are stable as a table, spiritual arts remind us that a foot sweep can take a leg out from underneath us. As Judokas, we learn to fall with grace when we find ourselves thrown. This is the art of allowing life to move us. This is Judo! We are taken from a place of being grounded to a place of groundlessness. This groundless place is the Second Life of Judo.

As we face all the unpredictable and choice-less difficulties that life provides, we can choose to accept and respond with kindness, or choose to resist and suffer. The unpredictable comes in so many forms. Today, it's problems with the kids, the dog, the in-laws, parents, or the weather. Tomorrow, it's our health, or the health of a loved one. When all is said and done, we realize we have no control over which experiences come to us in life and how they unfold. But we always have access to the present moment and can choose to be kind to ourselves.

"Identity *is thin.*"

STORY OF ACCEPTANCE

STORY OF ACCEPTANCE

I would like to share a short experience of acceptance and letting go of identifying with the ego. During the time I was injured, I had a dog named Weezy who was diagnosed with bone cancer. It was a sad and challenging time for my wife Gina and me, to see our beloved dog's physical decline. Soon after Weezy died, I adamantly told Gina that it wasn't the time for us to get another dog. I used my injury as an excuse. I was recovering from surgery and was in a lot of pain. I was fearful that I wouldn't be able to care for a new dog. Walking and bending was difficult for me. But something kept drawing my wife toward getting another dog, despite my pleas. As soon as she would get close to getting one, I would bark about my injury and rattle off numerous reasons why I couldn't properly care for a pup. Then, she would pull back. This little dance went on for a couple of months.

Finally, Gina said, "I will take care of the dog!" I thought, "This sounds like a pretty good deal. I will be able to love and receive love from another dog, and my wife will do all the hard work of raising a pup. What is there not to like about this deal?"

Shortly thereafter, we came home with Roxy, a beautiful Bullmastiff pup. Well, let me tell you how things developed from there. There is a fictitious character called Chucky from a horror movie series. Chucky is a doll that comes alive to cause death and destruction. Roxy soon (and rightfully) earned the nickname Chucky. She is what is known in the canine world as an alpha dog – the dominate one in her pack. Alpha dogs have great personalities, but require a lot of training.

I still felt very weak. Roxy sensed it, and took full advantage. Our battle of wills began as I tried to establish a healthy relationship with her. That relationship meant (to me): the human tells the dog what to do, and the dog is happy to please. Maybe I was still feeling a little shaken from the loss of my first dog. Maybe I was fearful that I would flare up my existing condition.

Either way, I knew I had to start with teaching Roxy: It is not acceptable to jump on my back, straddle my shoulders with her front legs, and take one of my ears in her mouth.

When Gina and I agreed to get a new dog, it slipped my mind that, since I was still healing and not back to work yet, I would be the one spending most of the day with Chucky (I mean Roxy). I remember taking numerous walks with her in the park, which turned into desperate wrestling matches for my gloves, hat, and the leash. On a few occasions, I would end up lying on the ground in a fetal position and in terrible pain, as Roxy ran around the field dragging her leash behind her. The look on her face suggested, "I have the prize – just try to get it back!" That prize, unfortunately, was my hat, and it was cold outside! She thought she could set the rules. But she was wrong.

After many weeks of blaming my wife for the situation, a transformation started to occur. I became aware of my energetic but unsatisfying reactions. I realized there would be no better time than that very moment to accept the situation entirely. I knew in my heart Roxy would never let me off the hook, until I accepted her and life just the way it was. I realized there is no such thing as "I will train Roxy when I start feeling better." Roxy became my teacher and taught me a spiritual lesson about presence. Naturally, I could have taken the heartless and easy way out, and given her away. But my wife and I loved her so much that it was not an option. I also intuitively knew that if I was to remove the hard work of training a puppy from my path, it wouldn't be long until another form of spiritual work showed up. As soon as I decided to accept Roxy and respond to her with unconditional love, our relationship changed.

In this case, unconditional love was a strict training routine. That was doing what was best for Roxy and what was best for me. I became a calm dog owner archetype, who established rules and boundaries, and Roxy slowly relinquished her Chucky-like habits. I knew: To be consistent with her training was what served her well and what served me well. The time to embrace the challenge of her was right then. Now, six years later, Roxy is well-behaved. As far as we can tell, she is balanced and happy. We now enjoy our walks in nature, without any hat stealing. Roxy taught me that suffering is directly related to resistance, and freedom from suffering is directly related to acceptance.

"Can your suffering diminish with great acceptance?"

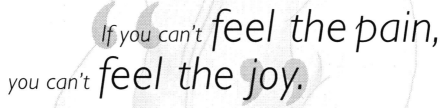

"If you can't **feel the pain,** you can't **feel the joy.**

—*Warrior Saying*

"The hard and stiff will be broken, the soft and supple will prevail.
—Tao Te Ching

THE FIRST LIFE
BECOMES THE SECOND

If you choose to climb the ladder of Judo belts – from the bright, light colors of white, yellow, and orange, to the deeper shades of green, blue, purple, brown, and black – you will inherit the journey of the Judoka. Putting a judogi over your shoulders and practicing the art may indeed infuse your life with spirit, but we are fortunate, in that, life itself is the perfect guide and sensei, providing us with all the lessons of spirit we will ever need.

The one question I am asked more than any is, "How Does One Enter the Second Life of Judo?"

The answer was handed down to me, and now it's my responsibility to hand it to you and wish you luck on your journey. The message has been spoken thousands of times, therefore it is no secret.

The message is truly universal and I believe could become accepted in every home in the world. It's not just a Caucasian thing, Far Eastern thing, Middle Eastern thing, African thing, British thing, European thing, male or female thing, Jewish thing, Christian thing, Muslim thing, or Buddhist thing: it is a *human* thing.

There comes a time in life, when caught in a predicament, that you look to the right and see nothing helpful there, and you look to the left and realize you have "been there, tried that." Then, feeling unfulfilled time and time again, you turn backwards only to see that the past won't help you out of this new jam. So, you attempt to move forward to figure your way out of this tight spot. Unfortunately, forward progress lands you smack down in the middle of hell. The money in your account doesn't help, your mother or father can't help, your reputation is meaningless, your lawyer and doctor say, "I'm sorry," and all your friends ask, "What can I do to help?" but you have no answer. Everything that you have accomplished and held up with your will power comes crashing down. Everything you are used to controlling seems lost. The bottom has just dropped out on the security and safety that you have known. This is the place of bearing weight. This is the "who, what, where, why, when, and how," when the Second Life of Judo first appears in your life.

The Second Life of Judo starts with a process of looking deep within; because you know in your heart no *thing* will answer the call. This is where the dark becomes light, the hard becomes easy, the impossible becomes possible, the helpless become helpful, the selfish become generous, and the cold become warm. This process of looking within is what I call "life work," because once it starts, it's an awareness practice we continue for the rest of our lives. The Second Life is a state of being that will carry you through all experiences.

I can only speak from my own experience, but the more I hear stories of transformation from others, the more waves of confirmation sweep over and sustain me. The content of our individual situations is unique, but the process of waking up to the peace beyond all understanding is universal.

In the Second Life of Judo, there is an awareness of the truth. Many more truths exist, of course, and it's an interesting and wonderful ongoing journey in discovery. But here is a partial list of truths that I hope you will find useful.

SECOND LIFE TRUTHS

We become more aware of how our mind works. We notice that we don't *have* to believe all the thoughts and stories of the mind.

We choose acceptance, by saying "yes" to the way things are right now at this very moment. All of life is welcomed to unfold, precisely as it does.

We are very grateful for so much richness in our lives, knowing that our time on this earth will be up shortly.

We are less compelled to chase after short-term gratifications, and therefore we can move out of cycles of addiction. We release the grip of attachments.

We are aware that the compassion we show to others is equal to the compassion we show ourselves.

If you are reading this book, you have started the process of inner development and transformation, from the First Life to the Second.

"What universal truth is calling you forward?
How do you live that experience?"

Conclusion

Before we develop our Judo skills, most of us spend a lot of time on our backs, trying to get out of holds or perfecting break falls. This introduction to Judo quickly leads to a crossroads. We must decide either to quit, or else become humble and continue. The very decision to show up for the next class is when the martial art becomes spiritual. Quitting may also be part of one's journey and may lead to wonderful outcomes. But showing up in the face of difficulty is practice at piercing the ego.

In the dojo, we learn to be free within the boundaries set by the sensei's authority. This is the true meaning of inner spiritual freedom. We adhere to the rules and rituals of the dojo, in order to see that freedom is an internal expression of spirit. We learn that our inner state of being does not rely on, nor is it determined by, external confines or conditions.

If the Sensei of Life makes you do push-ups, say "yes." Push-ups are necessary for muscle growth and absolutely necessary for spiritual growth. How else can we learn to say "Yes" over and over again? When we accept the hard things we have been transformed.

When I first started Judo, I always found the phrase "play Judo" kind of funny. I learned that the single word used most often in reference to practicing Judo, is indeed, "play." Judokas don't say "fight" Judo, "do" Judo, or "go Judoing." At first, it certainly didn't feel anything like "play" – having 185 lb. guys built like Rhinos, grabbing hold of me! I thought for sure my teacher was "playing" a bad joke on me. Now, over 30 years later, I have to say there really is not a better English word to describe this martial art. The more we "play" and practice Judo, the more we realize how "fight or flight" are not the only two options available to us. If we take time to notice the fight or flight reaction, we can tell it is one of resistance. We either ram into, or run away from, what we perceive as being threatening: two different ways of resisting "what is." Judo retrains our mind and body reflexes to relax and play with what enters into our circle of life. It's a middle way between fight and flight, a different and more spiritual tactic. We learn to play with everything, even with that which we fear. When the play occurs, a portal of possibility opens to something very spiritual. This is the awakening of the Second Life of Judo.

Judo has nothing to do with a tournament win over an experienced Judoka from another dojo. Judo is not about any title, credit, or praise. The martial arts are way bigger than any one specific style of teaching. It is nice when we feel a seemingly effortless technique in class, but Judo is really about how the practice shapes one's lifestyle. We practice Judo outside the dojo when we take time to just stop what we are doing, focus on the surrounding nature, then inhale, exhale, and enjoy. When is the last time you noticed yourself taking a deep belly breath? When is the last time that you noticed yourself staying still to feel the wind at your back? Something very special occurs when we merge with life in all its mystery. We allow this mystery to pull or push, and we respond. This is the Second Life of Judo.

The Second Life of Judo is not "better" or "graduated" from the First Life of Judo. The second is indeed not possible without the first. We may find ourselves in the Second Life of Judo when we can't stand up physically to the rigors of activity inside a dojo. We may find ourselves in the Second Life of Judo the moment we recognize that we no longer have to be enslaved by limiting thoughts. We may find ourselves in the Second Life of Judo when the Universe has given us another chance to be alive, just when we were sure that we were not long for this earth. Our Second Life happens *to* us, more so than *us* making it happen.

Keep practicing and playing Judo inside and outside of the dojo. May your dojo be your community and your home. Celebrate this moment as the only moment we ever have, the only moment there ever is – the moment that is now. This becomes your lifestyle of practice. This is the Gentle Way.

As in the Dojo, so in Life.

Small Warrior

Lower the head, lower the hands, honor the maker of the cloth...

Thumbs gently cover the bubbling spring...

The hurricane builds chi from the eye.

Graceful in entry; before Hajime bone touches bone.

Science of Defeat, one with the elements.

Spine now straight, gaze is empty.

Dojo door shuts, wind carries our favorite song.

Breath erases time.

— Zen Poem, Al

Glossary

ASANA: A yoga posture.

ASHRAM: The place where a Yogi lives and practices; a spiritual hermitage.

BODHISATTVA: One who vows to spiritually awaken others?

BUSHIDO: The "Way of the Warrior." A code of conduct related to a warrior class.

CHI: Energy flow or life force.

COME ON: An official invitation to step onto the mat, signaled by the sensei.

FENG SHUI: The Chinese system of achieving maximum harmony with one's environment.

GI: An abbreviation for Judogi.

HAJIME: Begin

JIGO HONTAI: A fundamental defensive posture initiated with the movement of one's hip, which is effective in stopping the Tori's throwing technique.

JUDOGI: The traditional Judo uniform used for practice or competition.

JUDOKA: A beginning student.

KESA-GATAME: The Scarf Hold, the first hold that is taught in Judo.

KIAI: A shout that gathers spirit.

Glossary

KOAN: A story, parable, riddle, question, or statement that cannot be understood by rational thinking. The meaning may be accessible through intuition or a personal experience.

KODOKAN JUDO: System of Judo from the founder, Kano. System of Judo taught at the "mother" school in Tokyo, Japan.

KUZUSHI: Unbalancing the opponent.

OBI: The Judo uniform belt.

ONSEN: A natural spring.

RANDORI: Free Practice. Free to move around the room and free to practice all techniques.

SENSEI: An authority who has mastered a craft.

TORI: A Judoka who is performing a technique.

TORII GATE: A traditional Japanese gate, which marks the sacred entrance to a temple or shrine.

UCHI KOMI: Repetition practice, with or without throwing.

UKE: A Judoka on the receiving end of a technique.

ZENDO: A meditation hall.

Mr. B and Al November, 1978 (left),
Al and Mr. B, February 2012 (right).

About The Author

Alan Rafkind has been a student of Judo for over 30 years. He's an avid reader, dog lover and enjoys the simple aspects of Life. He conducts interactive online classes via e-mail based on the information in this book and guidance handed down from his spiritual teacher. This book presents fundamental teachings of the art in a simple form, easily practiced by the layperson in order to enhance their quality of life. Alan currently resides in Matawan, NJ with his wife, Gina and their Bullmastiff dog, Roxy.

Alan can be found online at *www.thesecondlifeofjudo.com*